Maureen Duffy was born in 1933 in being a poet, playwright and novelist, she has also published a literary biography of Aphra Behn, and *The Erotic World of Faery*, a book-length study of eroticism in faery fantasy literature.

After a tough childhood, Duffy took her degree in English from King's College London. She went on to be a schoolteacher from 1956 to 1961, and edited three editions of a poetry magazine called *The Sixties*. She then turned to writing full-time as a poet and playwright after being commissioned to produce a screenplay by Granada Television. She made her debut as a novelist with *That's How It Was*, published to wide acclaim in 1962. Her first openly gay novel was *The Microcosm* (1966), set in the famous Gateways club in London. Among her later novels, *Gor Saga* was televised in 1988 in a three-part mini-series called *First Born*, starring Charles Dance, and *Alchemy* (2005) is now out in paperback from Harper Perennial.

Duffy has published around 30 other books, including five volumes of poetry. Her *Collected Poems, 1949–84* appeared in 1985. Her work has often used Freudian ideas and Greek myth as a framework.

She took an active part during the debates around homosexual law reform, which culminated in the Act of 1967. In 1977 she published *The Ballad of the Blasphemy Trial*, a broadside against the trial of the *Gay News* newspaper for 'blasphemous libel'.

She has also been active in a variety of groups representing the interest of writers, and is currently the President of the Authors' Licensing and Collecting Society, and a Fellow of the Royal Society of Literature. She is deeply interested in issues around enforcing traditional forms of intellectual property law, and is President of the British Copyright Council.

Maureen Duffy
Family Values

ENITHARMON PRESS

First published in 2008
by Enitharmon Press
26B Caversham Road
London NW5 2DU

www.enitharmon.co.uk

Distributed in the UK by
Central Books
99 Wallis Road
London E9 5LN

Distributed in the USA and Canada
by Dufour Editions Inc.
PO Box 7, Chester Springs
PA 19425, USA

© Maureen Duffy 2008

ISBN: 978-1-904634-60-7

Enitharmon Press gratefully acknowledges the financial support of
Arts Council England, London.

British Library Cataloguing-in-Publication Data.
A catalogue record for this book is available
from the British Library.

Designed in Albertina by Libanus Press
and printed in England by
CPI Antony Rowe, Chippenham Wiltshire

For Georgi

ACKNOWLEDGEMENTS

Some of these poems first appeared in the following publications: *Arts Council of Great Britain New Writing*, *London Magazine*, *Oxford Poets 2001* (Carcanet), *Pretext* (UEA), *Sightlines* (Vintage for RNIB), Torriano Press, *Writing on the Wall* (Weidenfeld & Nicolson). Some have been broadcast on BBC Radio 4.

CONTENTS

Blues Underground	9
Revenant	10
Reserved Occupation	11
Imprint	12
Progress	13
A New Christmas Carol	14
Salvage	15
Eirlys	16
Knickers	18
Game Birds	20
Revenant II	21
Paternity	22
Easter 1998	23
60th Remembering: June 14th 2005	24
Keys	25
Veneziana	26
A Sunday Outing	27
Cows Crossing	28
Phaeton	29
Quickstep	30
Wassail	31
Voices	33
Still Life with Pomegranates (1963) by Elizabeth Blackadder	34
The Stories of Old	36
On Reading Charles Simic's 'My Weariness of Epic Proportions'	37
Legend	38

A Wessex Farmer	40
Waiting for the Barbarian	41
Für Christoph	43
Lament for the Scribblers	44
Nightingales	46
Family Values	47
Silkie	48
Anniversaries	50
Monitors	51
Fashioned	52
Natural Selection	54
In Nova Scotia	55
Ogres and Augurs	60
Tourist Talk	61
Naming	62

BLUES UNDERGROUND

The blind man whistles at the foot of the stairs
while his stick taps out a pattering rhythm
on the side of the tin where he hopes
the pennies will drop. As the escalator
hurries me away I suddenly make out the tune
and I'm back in the school hall
staring up at the white cards held shakily aloft
by two big boys from top class, the words
painted in dark purple: 'Morning has broken
like the first morning', its whiff of Eden
a cloak for our childish aspirations:
the scholarship, the high school.

I want to go back and ask him, 'Why that?'
But I'm carried on and up, as we were
unless we fell by the wayside.
There were no guard rails, no safety net.
We were on our own, clinging tight
as the moving staircase propelled us
to some desired but not quite foreseen end.
So now this whistler in the guts
of the underground brings back Newtown Junior
Mr Meek, headmaster, exhorting us to praise
sunrise and the fresh morning as the hidden belt
carries me forward and up into the maw
of Liverpool Street station, and another journey back.

REVENANT

A quarter century on your ghost comes haunting back
squats on the blacker strip of verge picked out
by the headlights and I scramble again
ungainly after as you scuttle away
just as you did before, only this time
I don't come back in the frosty dark
to find you dropped askew, eye dulled. The guns
have been out all day cracking the frozen
silence. As you run from me one wing
tries to lift the other warped close
to the curve of your back. Pest, vermin
crop stuffer, country cousin yet smart
suited in your rose waistcoat, black tie
morning coat, unlike that poor townee
a car once slammed into my path, only
the unmourning stars will see you go out
your plump puffball kicked aside by the shot
while I sketch these obsequies for another
small, quenched, unrepeatable spark.

RESERVED OCCUPATION

Sad Jack, our cousin says you're lately dead who barely
lived. 'A good boy to his mother,' bronchitic, reserved
occupation, you saw to her while the last war
fell around you as the first had put paid to your father.
Always at family parties you were the quiet one
smiling as you passed the parcel or held a niece
or nephew on your knee while we sang of Kathleen
who'd never go home or the skylarking wife lost
in unclimbable reaches where angels tread water
and your mother shook her red cheeks in lieu of
those plump thighs she'd front line chorused with. If you
hankered for other places, people, Jack of a trade
but never master, it didn't show. For years, passing
entrained above Bromley junction, I'd trace the legend
Brown and Tawse, Precision Engineers, and think:
'That's Jack's firm.' *Toolmaker* gave you a sharper edge.
Retired, of a Sunday, your sister writes you'd retread
our Wenceslas steps to her front door. On Wednesday
the crematorium chimney will let you out
in short puffs shallow as your own breath, brief smudges
between sky and Essex flats; end of our district line.

IMPRINT

So these were the words that shaped me, here
in *The Big Christmas Wonder Book*, stuffed with
the sage and onion of stories and poems
my favourite festive fare, published when I was three
to celebrate a crowning that soon went awry.
At eight I crossed the snow-sheeted common
to find it, a paper grail, on my mother's cold
consumptive's bed where a nurse, a red-cloaked Santa
had left it. 'Your little girl likes reading, doesn't she?'

So here I find them again after
more than sixty years: the scullion
who won honour, the rats, he and she, who
ventured out after cheese and never came back.
Here I learnt how the winds swing the weather
through its compass of seasons and how
you should seize the moment and dance
to the grasshopper band before
they lay down their fiddles forever.

It's as if I was mapped in these pages with a template
I only had to follow to set my life in cold print.

PROGESS

Do you remember the soda jar, its heavy biscuit stoneware
that made it so hard to shake the right number
of glazed sugarcube crystals into the bowl
(licked they shrivelled your tongue)
and the knitted string dishcloth that went with it
that had to be boiled once a week or it grew slimy
and stank? Do you remember how your hands
were chapped red after, with white ridges
pleating your fingertips?

Now I stack the dishwasher, or you do, solo,
unpack and put away; not even a wipe
at glass clear as running water, without
the scum of soda, the dishcloth's greasy smears.
No regrets for those. Yet some perhaps
for the gossip over a shared task
as one washed and one dried.

A NEW CHRISTMAS CAROL

Christmas brought extra jobs. My aunt
all year long labourer about her house
whitening the front doorstep, at laundry
in the yard, when Yule came round
went out to work again, conjuring up
her single days or wartime in the polishing shop
where the wooden carriages were burnished to the gleam
of Rolls Royce facias, with singsongs
gossip, cracks on men and manners, the foreman's wiles.
Silvered with Santa dust they stacked the cards
by county, town and street, greetings across a bleak land
where the lavatory was still outdoors, bath
in the kitchen, coalite fires. 'Just once a year,'
she'd say, 'and that's enough, that journey
through the backchats to where me and my mate
were still girls, arm-in-arm on Monkeys' Parade
touching the boys up with our feather ticklers
as they sauntered past, until they turned to chase.'

SALVAGE

My mother's cutting-out shears were sacred.
I wasn't allowed to blunt their edge even
on pattern paper so flimsy it might
have been stuck on the sweet bottoms of macaroons
and be swallowed like secret messages.
I can see them now laid against the pattern edge
or the line from the grey coin of chalk that darkened
where I put my tonguetip to it, and the wooden
tabletop that had to be recovered
with a newspaper cloth for tea, carving
upper to lower with that unmistakable
grind against the wood, decisive, no going back
the length of the blades, those jaws too blackly
heavy in her bony fingers that held them
steady as a gun to the shoulder; now
nearly her lifetime away. They trimmed me
to my shape, snipped off my dry selvages
though others pinned and tacked, eased a seam or two.
It was her wielding of the shears, not those
she sometimes used that let fall triangular
confetti, small silk sails, tweed spores, black
beauty spots in serge, pinked out, but the fatal
severers that ground away what you must work with.
And I've been gathering ever since, smocking
shortening or lengthening hems and cuffs to get
a proper fit, something I can walk out in
not off the peg, ready made, but tailored
as she'd call herself, closing the metal jaws
resonant across the tabletop.

EIRLYS

Running down to winter the vines
put on a last spurt
tendril towards the sun
light harvesting, scrape October's
thin sky soup onto their green plates
and gorge before the first chill breath
fills their veins with dried blood.
Up with the larky radiocaster
I drive through morning twilight
past women statuesque at bus-stops
knowing I can't give a lift to them all.

Up betimes our foremothers, cycladic
thighs thickened by childbearing
and buttocky suet pudding
or spry draggletails, gran's army
of widows and those whose old men
weren't up to much, waited for trams
dreading winter's onset, out in the frozen dark
with stockings over their boots
to swab and flick a duster
before the office boys blew in
shooting their paper cuffs.

All over the world they are still rising
to slice snow from pavements
under my hotel window on a Moscow morning
clean carriages, polish boards for money
to walk over, wipe the seats
for other bums and flush, polish
the city's sole with elbow grease
and beeswax, holding back disorder

and the silting down of dust, time's
and weather's fingerprint on sill
or handle, forerunners of that last
slide into all our winters.

And I think of how we laid one in the earth
on a summer morning, celebrating the four kids
she raised alone, her five jobs to keep them
and how her tall sons' tears acclaimed
her membership of those secret
battalions that might sweep the old
order away. She was called Eirlys.

One Sunday dinner time she spelled it
for me on the pub table in spilt beer
that old name of a white flower
from her native mountains and woods.
Slim still as an asphodel
poking up through the dust
she would have taken pan and brush to.
Her life held up to the light
seems full of bright motes dancing.

KNICKERS

My granny got up at six to go out cleaning
that's why I suppose she used to say:
'Best place in the world is bed,'
not thinking the last place in the world is bed too.
Her children mocked her, hooked on dancing
as they were on silk knickers and vests.
They tried to prize her out of her itchy
knee-length woollen drawers. Later my mother
would say it killed her but cancer is no considerer
of knickers. It got her finally six months
before I was born, another of those I never knew
but have her snapshot laughing with two
of her daughters, my aunts, Dodger who died
in her twenties out of the shed put up
in the East End garden for the family
consumptives so they could breathe their full
ration of soot (was she 'my little dark daughter'
my granny fretted over as the anaesthetic
took her down for the operation she
never came through? Or was it my mother
unmarried, pregnant with me in lodgings
in a distant seaside town?) and Ada
(Minge was her family name) the cleverest
of them all, smart as a grammar school girl
and out of the san for the first time in years
killed by an axis bomb, the first casualty
in that little coastal town. Grace, my mother
never forgave Hitler. She liked her bed too.
Not that she ever got much of it except
when packed off to the sanatorium
in her turn. Otherwise she was always early
up and about. So now when I want to linger
in the companionable warmth of bed

all of them get me up and going
crying out of the past: 'We're a long time
dead' with a ritual of bath and briefs on.
('You'll catch your death in those,' they
would have said.) And breakfast, putting off
that moment when I shall lie down with them.

GAME BIRDS

In flight from the guns on the hill
the smart pheasants have come down to flock
about the gardens. I count fifteen before
they scuttle away from the spectral face
at the window, my careless sudden shift.

Tortoiseshell-back, wet-sand breasted, the hens
pick among the gravel where there seems
not a grain of sustenance, while the cocks
gaudy as cousinly peafowl strut their stuff
with avian shrieks and football-rattle
gobble. Jockeying for place or sex
they face each other down, ducking, bobbing
their jewelled heads, ruby, ivory, jet
and sapphire till one backs off.

On the hill, dogs and beaters scythe on
methodically, putting up those who
didn't dare the descent. They stagger
into the air, stout, not fashioned for flight
but for potshots. At early twilight
two trucks head down the track cargoed
with dun corpses, anonymous butcher's meat.

REVENANT II

Turning the corner today, uphill, going somewhere else
quite by accident, I suddenly see the Twelve Bells –
the low wall, the forecourt, then the name of the street
and I think: I lived here once, 'after the war'
when I was twelve, wheeled my bike along the concrete path
to the gate so I could fly, feet off the pedals
freewheeling to school, looked out of that upstairs
window to fields beyond Cherry Orchard Estate
where the sunset burned with promise of shine tomorrow.

And have never been back since, two years later
my stepfather carried my case to the station.
Now it's New Year's Day again, another beginning
and that old, old ending stares me down
from its bleak window with the torn rag of curtain
from a time when days dragged slow feet
through every minute to this now of fled
and flying years and I know I can never go back.

PATERNITY

Well Dad, with you long dead
or maybe somewhere knocking on a century
I stumble across a late understanding
served up by a garrulous taxidriver
Paddy from Sligo, about the old IRA
you claimed to be serving seventy years ago
that it wasn't just as we always thought
a con trick to dodge the wedding band
you should have fingered my mother with
but a real prohibition.
'Jesus, you can't marry a Prod
while you're in the Army, if ever.'
Not then that you wouldn't
but couldn't, and that plaisters
some of the old wound, shrapnel slivers in the flesh
leftovers from a long dead war.

And not that I let it bleed me to death
though always sharp to your absent presence
seeing you in strange men on the bus
and saying in my head, 'We don't need you'
yet alive to the fables and songs
that are half of my heritage.
Now I'm glad to be credulous
wanting to believe your part in me wasn't
just the dancing deceiver we took you for
slinging his gun from the bedpost
but as well the one who peeled the little brown shrimps
for his lover with finicky patience
(though he couldn't put his bike back together)
and registered my name as your own
so everyone should know I wasn't stillborn
Dad or Da, whichever and wherever you are.

EASTER 1998
for Lil and Michael

I ring you from across the water.
'The champagne's nearly gone,' you say
the lovely pop of peace
the gas of gladness
incandescent through the veins.

It runs like an older story.
'And when they wouldn't listen
those barrack room lawyers
with children's blood on their hands
the queen, Mebd, threw her wig at them
took her cloak of suffering about her
and went to speak to those mazed men of terror
whose crime was believing in fables.'

All that was long ago
yesterday
in the land of missed and bogged down.
This morning breaks with the clarity of ice.
Now we must learn to meld these bright fragments
into one clear pane.

60TH REMEMBERING: JUNE 14TH 2005

Beside the railway track the oxeye daisies
are open for business, the fireweed
tosses its willowy head whose small flames
once cauterised the wounds of the blitz.
Yet seared flesh and spirit still suppurate
under scar tissue letting out a thin seep of pain.
So my remembrance today is of my aunt
Ada, the clever one, on remission
from the airy sanatorium to convalesce
in our front room and, after the bomb fell
laid out on the cold pavement, as my mother
later told me. Someone had given her
a wad of gauze that she dabbed at her wounded
forehead, unaware of the shattered legs below
and crying: 'Let me go with them.
I want to go with them.'

KEYS
H. B. 1913–1985

'Darling, I've dropped my keys. Can you let me in?'
Your voice would mole up muffled by the entryphone.
I'd dredge myself from whatever midnight oil I'd
been sousing in to scrabble the duplicates out
of their envelope, labelled in your script. 'Darling,'
the only man who ever called me that, 'It's most
frightfully kind,' when I'd stumble downstairs to find
you upright, just, your lips gleaming a little
as though you'd run a preparatory tongue tip
to oil them for Hardy. 'Us coloured chaps,' you'd claim
whose father governed tea-leafed Ceylon, slim still in
Hamlet blacks and proud of it, your skin pinking while
we sparred round after round and you tried for a double
conversion. I've still got your keys though you've gone off
for good. The heirs won't need them, yet I can't throw them
away. So I let them lie in the box with your hand
fading, and if in the end you are right: there's
a gate, with a keeper sour from forever trawling
the human lake, I shall say, 'Look I still have
Hughie's keys,' and hear your high Thespian camp as
they take them in: 'Darling, how frightfully kind.'

VENEZIANA
for JJN

Surely the city must finally sink without you.
When I tuck in to my pizza veneziana
(ten pence from every one for the perilous fund)
in a ristorante on homeground West London
and raise my glass of Montepulciano
housewine elegante, spear up
pine kernels more reminiscent
of Dante's Florence (all Italy's here
to musak by Monteverdi) admire
the masked, masquing candle, brilliant
in its fake Murano stained-glass shield
I can see a rightness in Norwich and Venice
linked by better than their football teams
and you more apt than Canute in keeping
the waves at bay with words or a finger or two
in the dyke, plugging the gaps with passion
and lucre, staking the city's roots
in concrete so it can stay afloat
islanded, the drifting, gilded
featherbed of our dreams.

A SUNDAY OUTING

'I knew if anyone could find me out you would,'
Your cracked lips force the words through, bloody drop by drop.
I say I'm sorry. Hope you don't mind.
A private person who never quite came out, always on top

except with one or two, including me. 'It takes
one to know one.' Today I've driven through weeping rain
and howling wind to find you here; past infernal lakes
the season fills from every open city vein.

The gaunt old hospital's about to close; the new post-modernist
gleams in brick and tile but no one sleeps there yet.
Instead it's still this seamy block, the scabrous lift
that hauls me up alone to an unmarked floor where I'm met

a little curiously, I think. The nurses' eyes
outshine in semi-precious jet or opal; tongues soothe
with creole and blarney. Yet their smiles can't disguise
the bagged bones the masseur comes with gentle touch to smooth.

I turn the corner and see you lying so flat it's as if
they've let out all your air. Or like the pictures in the Tate
they were queuing for as I drove past: no third dimension, no relief
plain pain, sans serif. Mortality's at best a dodgy state.

But here there's love enough to break your heart.
I take your hand. This thin the wrist bends back on a bone
Hansel might have thrust through the caging bars. We don't know
                                    how to part.
Instead I ask and hear how long you've known.

COWS CROSSING

Round the corner I brake, the tarmac ahead
become a comber of cows, a flash flood of flesh
a surge of fluid black and white boulders
their legs gaunt trestles for the bagpipe
of cream that threatens to topple them
shoehorns skittering on their own slurry
yet whose gait's somehow graceful, measured
two by two like schoolgirls in a crocodile
or eternal children holding arms or hands
with ribbons in their forty-year-old shingles
and draggletail print frocks, out for a treat.

They cross with the sideways seesaw of hammocks.
Sometimes a head turns to look at my throb of car
checking the flow a moment, then wedges forward again
to follow, knowing I have no answers
just that twice a day she must cross from one
mud-puddled field to another as long as she lives
blessedly not foreseeing as I do the bolt
for captives, the pithing rod: Aditi
wetnurse to us all come down to this ponderous
pendulous presence on the road that too briefly
breaks my journey with her gangling epiphany
momentary damascene incised on a grey morning
piercing, pierced.

PHAETON

That morning you didn't feel like tennis.
Now I learn your brilliant silhouette
elegant as a dancer, has been whited out
erased in a day by swirling particles
that boiled then froze your beautiful brain
as if you had stepped outside into a blizzard
and can never be found again.

Still your friends' thoughts finger your tall imprint:
dandy, duellist with a blade of wit, courtier
or Restoration prince I met that day
of mourning and have celebrated ever since
remembering your daguerreotype framed
by your skyey flat high over town
slim fingers serving our supper, music, wine.
You dared to borrow the sungod's chariot
and are fallen forever, down, down.

QUICKSTEP

Pregnant at 28
bombed out at 34
buried a second time and for good at 42
Today it's 56 years since that morning
you fell down on the pavement
and the blood drowned your breath
or was it your heart? I wasn't there.
Sent away not knowing the real why.
But you knew. Must have or why did you sunder us
with a hundred miles, sparing me that fall
for your sake as well as mine.
The year is turning again on beech and chestnut.
The dark comes in too soon and stays too late.
You would want me to keep the lights on
while I can, playing those tunes
your crumpled feet sang to: foxtrot, quickstep, tango
until the last waltz before midnight.

WASSAIL

Off to bury Ivy I run through the platitudes, close
cousins to those doldrums where our ship founders or's becalmed.
The tube shuttles me from West to East, present to past
an unpaid bill trolleying across Button and Clemoe's
outfitters, under two thousand years of London embalmed
above, around me; a century of it ours. Upcast
at Bethnal Green each stop's a grey-felted scrapbook page:
snapshot Bow where I was first schooled to read and write; Plaistow's
chest clinic whose Little Titch doctor told me to eat my greens.
Beyond Barking's pot-bellied gas retorts my glass cage
looks out on scrubby country till Dagenham's soiled quest
for urbs in rure, flat fields slicked back with rain
where the wind keens and I'm almost there.

You didn't suffer like some, had all your marbles
unchipped as the flawless glass jewels, ruby, emerald,
sapphire or crystal with a barley sugar core
we ricocheted down the gutter or your string
of clear beads, had fourscore years and then
a bit of a cold or less. Nothing
to worry about, a case for aspirin and camphor.
But everything happened to you at Christmas: married
widowed, so it's somehow right that we're here again, three days
to go, the kings on their way, the Sally Army oompahing
through the shopping mall and none of your cards sent. Harried
by a rain bitter as old men's dewdrops, in saffron clays
that clog our boots, we stand with smart plastic grass cladding
the indecent mounds, and learn your hidden life. You came
here every week for twenty-six years bringing children, then
grandchildren so they should know and there'd always be flowers

to his name. There's a gap on the stone where a flame
can burn your reticence between husband and brother.
Your middle-aged children hang on to their lovers
as though they might slip and teeter in
where the family grave lies wetly agape.

And it's Christmas I recall with us coming
on Boxing Day through mist and snow
to where you were living then with a stop for rum
and coffee at the station buffet before the chill
always downhill stroll to welcome: the crates brought out
roast, sprouts and spuds and beer, the games and singing
to a lone piano. Whispers we played, Musical Chairs
Pass the Parcel. Then it was each in turn to solo: Danny Boy
I'll be Your Sweetheart, take you home my dear, my all
while you and your Roy in the kitchen were stoking us
up stairs with cups of tea loose laced with gin
till time was called for aunties two in a bed, a cousin
sandwiched between. And suddenly I'm stormed
by all the things I wanted to ask gone with you
into the family plot, sucked down by those wet lips.
The last repository of ways pre-war; in service, first you
then him, uniformed by scratchy serge battledress
'It was hot as hell but I learned to drive a truck
though I was jittery at first.' Lord of his milkfloat
smashed to bits on Christmas morn.

Indoors again, the family word for home, I find
wedged in the tread of my soles thick tears of clay.
I get a knife, a potted plant, pale refugee, leggy with winter blues
and scrape their earth I can't just throw away
into the fired clay and tamp it down.

VOICES

'You shouldn't dwell on the past,'
they said, as if it was a high plateau
arid, windswept, of bitten grass
stones for bread, scant dew to drink
or a door opening into the ravished house
with only entrails of pipes, a cistern
a lavatory pan left dangling like some
installation piece entitled despair.

They knew its hallucinatory power
how witchwise the past could clutch you to it
draw you under the hill or down, down
below green waters and how they are
always there, the half glimpsed mist-wraiths
the voices, echoing in a favourite phrase
a cadence, so the gut lurches again with loss
even after half a lifetime. They knew all that
the old wives: how green girls could sicken
and fade with too long greeting over a grave.

So we dreamed up Ever After, Everlasting
while the voices cry out with Dido's bleak
plangency: 'Remember me, remember me.'

STILL LIFE WITH POMEGRANATES (1963) BY ELIZABETH BLACKADDER

Those Persephone pips, did you eat them
after the life was dismantled
the last drain from the white jug cat-lapped
the empty coffee pot black as Stephenson's
Rocketing smokestack back on the stove
then lay yourself down to dream
on the hot striated rug?

We live flatly, patterned on time
you seem to say, and that renascence
discovery of 'the art of prospective in scenes'
is just a trick of theatre conjured
by wavering footlights, the tawdry costumes
and masks to keep the children glamoured
forever on the edge of their seats.

Here it's as if there were no beyond or below
only our ancient or quotidian
artefacts at rest on a white ground.
You paint perfection of petals
in bruised iris and flagging tulip.

Yet these succulent squares are seeds
that might drop roots or lift stems
and there's no Lazarus rising
without dying, going down into dark
beyond Demeter's reach, sunk into
those gloomy arms below your painted
surface of what we have and can only lose.

Beyond the window are hills, waters
to look out on; land and seaskips
your gaze also flattens till they become
more than themselves, paysages for voyaging.
Always what isn't there resonates through.
This is the language of spaces, white nights'
omissions you lay your jewels against
to burn evenly. Demeter when she descended
pleaded on her knees in the world of shades.

'How many,' the black king asked her daughter,
'have you eaten?' That half dozen, crunched
til the juice ran, kept her in darkness
and us too six months of the year.
Was it love held her down? She might have risen
into the upper light and air. They were only
fruit after all. You've painted seeds enough
for oblivion. They thrust their shoots
piercing the bright surface; and we are
shot through, bruised with Hades' heel.

THE STORIES OF OLD

Slaying dragons must always have been a part-time job
finding the right sort of cave or picking up
the bottled message on the shore sent by a mutinous
princess, who refused to make a roast dinner
and with no compensation for scorching
or a broken skull from a giant's clout.
Ogres must have been few and far between
and royalty pinch-penny for all your efforts.

So when it came time to hang up your sword
it was off to the monks to take you in
or the hermit's dank cell with only your old nag
for company, cropping at the cave mouth
spavined with years, a grey muzzled dog, and a cat
with toasting-fork ribs; that's if you were lucky.

But old man Blake gave the questing life
his imprimatur, like our school hymn that
set me up with imaginary spurs still clattering
in the dust as I hobble on. Somewhere
I mislaid my steed but dog and cat lollop
along beside me. And I was luckier than most.
I got to keep the princess. She stirs my pot.

ON READING CHARLES SIMIC'S
'MY WEARINESS OF EPIC PROPORTIONS'

But she couldn't of course even with her mother's sayso.
Going down that little path through the vineyard
with the birds shouting that the war was over
the amphora a diadem balanced on her high head
she should have expected that one of the drunken soldiery
would leap out between the cornrows of vines
bear her down, the amphora falling on the springy thyme
like her not broken but bounced, her cries
stifled in the white flowers of wild garlic.
She'd say it was Jove up to his tricks again
like all virgin births with nothing
but a god for a father and she was hoping
to be reft skywards if no one would take on
the twins with complementary birthmarks
an arrow and a spear to raze more cities.

LEGEND

They aren't at all as we've imagined them
these events at the top of the tall house
whose lower rooms dealt in import and export
invoice and ledger and bill of sale
between the duck-dipped canals.
It's the father who comes back
Ulysses to us, wagging an old dog's tail
thump, thump of recognition and hope
not knowing his wife, children, friends
have all charred in Moloch's gullet.
We watch with him while hope gutters out.

History is at best fiction, what we choose
to pluck and preserve. There were eight people
up there, terrified or resigned
the ugly, the undesired, the peevish
the Lazarus who returned
to a life still sepultured.

'Of the girls who died, most of them Trojan
from rape and the sword, we remember
Iphigenia who greased the slipway
with wine-dark bubbles dashed from her maid's veins.'
Myth cleanses history of slime and terror and ash.

And those who stripped to their blond skins
to bathe in Phlegeton, trusting
Persephone would bring them
pomegranates to suck to the domed husk
(with thin red juice running down their chins
as they licked their fingers of immortality)
time's flushed them away too, leaving

this icon of a schoolgirl bent
over her diary, and each of us
murderer and preserver running up the stairs
while we beg the huntsman not to cut out
Snow White's heart as the pencil whispers
an older story: 'Once upon a time
there was a princess. The wolf ate her.'

A WESSEX FARMER

Now down the lane he'll come no more landroving
driving his seventy-odd years of pain
or stop to chat, limbs harrowed by tines
of labour, face furrowed by wind and rain.

Oh spread it thick in *Farmer's Weekly*
broadcast it on the internet
Philip whose roots were Aetlardus, Domesday
is now in those same flint beds set.

Deep in the ground he ploughed and sowed
where fox and badger can't take revenge
where corn and stock prices won't fall further
his twice-mended knees at last unhinge.

Noble and brave were his forefather's names
who farmed these downs when Alfred thrashed the Danes.

WAITING FOR THE BARBARIAN

We are dining above the city
in your top flat looking down
on Hampstead trees and grass. You have cooked
cauliflower cheese, potatoes, mushrooms
and marmalade cream. You down your whisky
I my driver's tot of red.

Your mind's eye's as sharp as ever
though you worry about your sight.
Reading's sometimes a strain
When you go to fetch our pudding
you hand yourself from chair to
sideboard to doorhandle but won't
let me leave my seat.

We gnaw on politics, your faith
fresh still though you pare away
the shams with your sharp edge.
Does he mean it, you ask; do I
believe? I say I do, wanting to
but doubt what we shall contrive
without the bogeyman to get us
into our clean pyjamas upstairs
to bed. You laugh and quote
at once Cavafy.

We talk of going back to your first
drafts around your autumn birthday
of you enthroned in the mayor's
parlour. They'll lend you his black Rolls
to ferry you about the city
you once garnished with golden
promises and your love.

I make my way down your bare flight
and outside under the charcoal
doodles of March branches look
back up at the windows where
you are waiting with dignity
the coming of the great barbarian
when the orators will make
their speeches while the rest of us
stand seriously.

Hanging over the banisters
to wish me goodnight, needing just
ten more runs for your century
you smile from the border as if
to reassure that although
the barbarian is always squatting
in that darkness beyond the frontier
we mustn't fear. He will come
in his own bad time.

FÜR CHRISTOPH

Taking off my new black vest
bought against a cold snap in your handsome city
I see a powdering of small scales
sloughed by my skin in a day.
Every seven years they tell us we moult completely
so this is the beginning of my eleventh hour
an autumn velvet like stags before winter.
This morning we passed between golden age landskips
where the fist of frost never clenched
through the romantic fallacy of forever
lemon tree country. The ruins of lost worlds
stared down from the gallery walls where we were treading in talk
side by side with Goethe and Coleridge
through sunset in the Sabine Hills.

LAMENT FOR THE SCRIBBLERS

Poets should be better at winter, not drop
like the tarry stares that feathered the telegraph wires
in October as if they had somewhere
to be going when we knew they would still
mump about the backyard for a crust till a clear night
cut them down to a tatterdemalion frieze
of starched black quills, relics of those too cocky
whose sad plumes are tacked to the tarmac
with paste of blood and bone yet stir in the traffic draught.

Pupil and master in one week's too much.
We're not prepared although we knew the score: ninety
hoar years must soon come down to dust; drink
and despair will do for the best. The coffin
wardrobe slams its door on soft shell suits keeping
a buried shape; abandoned triangle coathangers
jangle their wiry discord; shoes down at heel
lie quiet at the back in a caul of fluff.
The fedora is finally laid blackly away.

Given the choice which would we take: five years
of life in death at the full end before the frost's sharp snip
sans peur and everything or a lifetime's
dry gethsamene of fear begging for the cup
to pass our lips with its mulled oblivion
the unshed words festering in the closed throat
that only opens to engorge the truth spat out
so often and accurately, a green goblet
that cried for live coals not the put down of gas.

'It gave me up,' it's said you said, and there
your finger's on the button for us all, us scribblers
sinking through muddied middle age. No wonder
that we yearn to those who keep on: Hardy
taking the muse to his grave and the vicar
of nowhere, spare as sheep's bones, disdaining hafod
summer pasture, to turn a field of flint.
Last week at a rare reading I saw his hands shake
but from age or rage I couldn't tell
or Dunbar's *timor* that jostles all elbows

except those lovers of the moon goddess
sustained by starlight. Tell us you ghosts, paddle over
Tartaros with hindsight, hot news to wrap
our chips, while we shuffle on the sullen shore
our pockets crackling with obsequies to bribe
wisdom out of your lines and lives.
All winter we've teased you with memorials
unwilling to let you go. Now become
only your paged words, true body of your resurrection.

NIGHTINGALES
for Dulan

Poking the papery bulbs into thin London grit
that sand-papers skin like the bottom
of a galvanized bath, an earth we used to share
(you by adoption, me by descent) just as we had
our October birthday in common, so hated
the drawing in of autumn, the first fist of frost
as much as you loved light over a lagoon, parrot
tulips jutting green beaks into Spring, Mozart, ebony notes
things it's hard now to enjoy without your indelible voice
chiding and praising by turns; I thrust each memory
deep down with a corm barky as liquorice root
or the mandrake tubers of dahlias you used to conjure
into chinese lanterns to blaze against
the black scurf that clogs this time of year.

The heart constricts with pain and its palliatives
since we stood upright and saw on bowed and trembling legs
these farther shores, and plucked a leaf to ruminate on
blur our new awareness of gone or to come
barring the night with song to keep the dark away
as we two did across two decades setting disc or tape
unreeling our loves, griefs, hopes into the night.
Returning again three years on I find
your absence as presence still inhabits the house.
We speak of you often those who love you, carefully
as if we might wound ourselves. Oh our dear
as long as we live there will always be
music and flowers that bloom you against Fall, our dank October:
Heraclitus' nightingales awake and singing.

FAMILY VALUES
Homage to François Villon

It'll never get better if you pick it
You eat a peck of dirt before you die
Every cloud has a silver lining
Beauty's in the beholder's eye.

Everything comes to him that waits
You'll change your tune when you wed
It's a poor heart that never rejoices
Never say die till you're dead.

As long as you die a good colour
You must walk before you can run
You won't go till your number's up
Half a loaf is better than none.

One swallow doesn't make a summer
Pride comes before a fall
Time and tide wait for no man
The weakest go to the wall.

SILKIE

Pain off the front page where the seal people
suffer their saga in engrained silence
gape their grief on our breakfast tideline
sleek oilskins tarred and feathered by gannet
guillemot, scoter while we traitors scoot
Scott free. These wilds should be white fleeced
polar pure as bear pelt, ermine, snowy owl
breasted, chime with clear ice, not this
rancorous spew from the earth's dark bowel.

White world that was our dreamtime on the edge of things
Thule we have smirched and soiled, once upon
your people stepped through the neapflood, beached
and shed their skins, folding them hidden
under stones or in deal cupboards, to dance
with our sons and daughters on the sands
til they would need them again to take
our children or lovers back to the sea
to those coral and mother-of-pearl chambers
we knew they had always prepared for us.

Now sheer seadogs who should be puppying
in the waves, your coats cling like shrouds to your flesh
weigh you down in your element, sinking
through moted deeps where slicked sea otter
and sunken voyagers have gone before
Davy Jones locks up the park at night
and the silent tides tumble weed and wrack
and wreck. Your blunt heads nose in the silt

harpoon heavy, over and over
not gambolling but falling down to the soft seabed
and the salty silence stoppers your ears.

Great Silkie of Sule Skerri, have we gone
too far this time? Will you never come back?

ANNIVERSARIES

There's nothing special about September
slung between August and October
the month my mother died, the month
we met, so that this time each year
I swing between grief and hope. Summer
brought drought, dearth. Now the fields' cracked lips
suck down the autumn rain. In the lane
where the badgers hold their underground estate
late sun has painted a still-life to stock
the birds' winter larder with bloodied
elder swags and misted wet-slate sloes
against Ravilious backdrop
folds of pale ochre hills, striped and blotched
with the umbrous green of hedge and tree
colours from childhood's flat paintbox
its fairy cakes of cobalt, viridian, burnt sienna
in their white enamel tray with a black lid
that, all mixed together, become winter's sludge.
Now these late rains bring a greening. Grass sprouts.
Wild toadflax and tamed foxglove shout:
'It's not over yet; rejoice.'

MONITORS

The blackbirds are building again
my Spring monitors, urban cousins
of Clare's thrushy minstrels, twining
a nest perilous above catreach
strung among fronds of bitter ivy.
Are they the same pair every year?
How long does a blackbird live
if it isn't clawed out of life or run down?
When he chorales from a chimney pot
you can just hear the answer
from the old cemetery walks
a trafficked mile away.

Prodigal parents, they raise brood
after small brood to be tipped over
by a cat's paw on their first lopsided
launch while the old ones chatter
in shrill warning or encouragement.
Now that the sparrows no longer
high-rise in the eaves, fossick
or flurry their dusty feathers
in the common gutter, they're all
we have left as neighbours
when the pale spume of prunus
veils the cold March branches.
Except for the woodpigeons
those immigrants stout in smart
suits of grey with collar and tie
and the scavenging gulls, old salts
come ashore to ride the city thermals
and remind us that somewhere there's still the sea.

FASHIONED

It's the maid's furniture we lust after now.
Not the veneered Sheraton she coveted
and was bought when she wed but the blond pine
of her backstairs attic washstand, bosomy
chest-of-drawers, blanket box from a sailor father
that pressed her clothes into service on the top
of the carrier's cart, stripped, as she was
in the parky bedroom to wash with cold
jug and basin we fake afresh an attar
of blue roses twined in remembrance
her bodice falling in a frill about her waist
the soft pale calf emeried with goose pimples
by frost curtaining the panes with her light breath
while beyond and below loured armoire, escritoire
in timber solid as dark oak naval bottoms.

Her sudsy innocence has become
the furnishing of our dreams as we switch
channels conjuring visions remotely, shuttles
soar us to Glasgow or past the moon
the boxed particles bombard our dinners
to tender. She blew on sticks and paper
humped coals upstairs in a bucket
the antique market displays so polished
she could have seen her face in its brassy sun.
When she married she left, going home
to learn her children to break the ice
in the jug and wash behind their ears.
She shopped for the rich conker of layered
mahogany teaching us there's nothing new
under the all-consuming sun. Blued Brits
swapped grain and tin for smooth red kitchenware
and wine. We try to kindle new fire

our of her raked embers. As she took
her bedtime candle up the cottage stairs
the flame bending above the china stick
did she remember the varnished deal
of maidenhood and wonder how they were
managing without her up at the house?

NATURAL SELECTION

In the pheasant world Brown is boss.
After their head to head, not for my sport
watching through the window, but another notch
for Darwin or who dares wins
Blue, pale backed as a winter sky
stalks off shaking his carmine wattles
uncocksure. Their power play seems a game.
The steel claws don't rake each other's throats.
It's more a ballet of Nijinksky leaps
entrechats and truculent cries as they try
to do each other down without blood.

So is Blue denied treading a soft downy ride
or does he sneak back when Brown swans
off defending his range, distracted?
Do the hens think, 'Well why not?
Just in case … Like he's quite pretty really.
That Brown is a bit of a bully.'
And life's carried on by fine feathers
survival of the fittest by stealth.

IN NOVA SCOTIA
for E. B.

1. Spencer's Point

In your country where we have been holidaying
for health and truth, our guide leads us
cunning as a good Indian following
eyes down, the spoor of your dropped words.
Every stone is precious on this beach
where the shore tumbles constantly
marrying the sea with garlands of shrubs
saplings to lie among the uncut matrices
big as rocs' eggs, speckled red and white
white and ochre, striated like the islands
we made for geography in plasticine, ribbed
with a compass point or simply dappled
with 'amethyst, rose,' or freckled obsidian, tiling
fit for an emperor's floor.

. You can hear the tide turn across
the suck-you-down red mud mounds
with a distant drumming. The birds begin
to fly back as the cockles and lugworms
surface. 'Look, they're sandpipers'
obsessively sweeping the shore
probing with crescent beaks for sustenance
like us. But we turn back to the car
with our freight of stones, you knew
might have handled, needing, or not, water
or words to make them give back pattern, colour.

2. Duk-duk
for Charlie

Meeting us at the airport
held in your father's arms
you identify a flat glass mosaic
penguin or parrot
hung in a giftshop window
duk-duk
but then later a fish, a rose, a boat
even me
duk-duk.

Such a hard mythical coming
you had of it
your mother, sliced like a ripe fruit
to pod you out
you became miraculous overnight
cached in your glass cage
cocooned in serpenting tubes
that feed lungs and veins
where not long since
you both would have died.

Now we admire the perfect knees
that nudge you from room to room
so fast you're out of sight and into harm
a dozen times a day, the long scarves
you weave of bird calls,
practising sentences, songs, laments
and the precision of that other
pinpoint common noun
duk-duk, duk-duk.

3. At Chocolate Lake

I swam eight lengths between
the marker twins, alternating
blue and pink floats. Swimming's like
riding a bike: it all comes back
and there you are much where you left off
neither the worst nor the best.
A cruciform girl floats on her back
the pale kelp of her hair spread out behind
while boy efts who might be her brothers
duckdive dredging up coke bottles
weighted with chocolate sand
as if they were pearled oysters.
The black dog's owner wants him to swim too.
She drags him by the chain to the chill edge
but can't cajole him to have fun. He trembles
on the brink, his liquorice lips drawn back
on jaws that yawn with fright as if
to keep his old teeth from chattering loose
in the silver flecked muzzle. The cocoa silt's
all stirred up with overnight rain
threatening again from stained
mattress clouds. The eldest boy dropping
coined wet splodges across the sand
shouts the younger ones ashore, puts on
authority with his white bermudas, towels
their damp skin. Far out, nearly
at the island twin seal heads bob
while their son on his hands and knees
combs the shallows for pebbles
polished and coloured marbles
to suck on his sore gums. Suddenly

a swordfish, black and silver
a streak of wetsuit, goggle-eyed
but all of seventy, submariners
with twirling fins my poor lengths
at twice the speed, nimble as a killer whale.
The Japanese mother, eyes down, follows
her brisk young daughter, second generation
delicately, to paddle in the unheeding waters.

4. At Murphy's

'Why, why do we feel
(we all feel) this sweet
sensation of joy?' *The Moose*

We hire a boat or rather pay our ticket
cockleshell, light blue two-decker, one up
one down, too frail for whale watching
a flick of the tail would have us turned turtle.
It has to be a con but we climb aboard
over the gut-heaving gunwhale
past postcard seagulls corking up and down
on the briny billows, through waters
dark blue to starboard, creamier whisk to port.
It's so easy to become nautical
to be swept up, down, along or below
with behind, our thousands of years, navigating
islands, continents, skimming salt water.
Almost I could believe in 'something in the blood'.

We pass rocks that are beached whales
or resting elephants, grey, smooth and huge:
a bellbuoy topped with its photofit gull;
run the darkly conifered shoreline
until suddenly a gun-grey navy boat
trailing its blue scarf wake, threatens to run
us down. But no Moby fountain, tail fin
big as a mill sail rolls out of yesterday's
rumour of a sighting, a spouting.

The radio crackles. There are porpoises
if we can reach them in time, cavorting inshore.
Our captain turns about and I can't judge
whether it's not to disappoint the customers
us, or because he too wants to see
as we do peering, dazzled against
the corrugated steel sheets of the inlet's waves
backs rising in a shaving foam
porpoises dancing out of the water
humping themselves, their striped hides, into view.
'We're here, follow, follow. Watch us.'
And we do. All leaning, exclaiming, snapping.
'It's lucky,' I tell you, dredging the legend
up from some seabed. 'He won't remember,'
his mother says, holding her year-old son
against a thwart. 'Look at them, look. Porpoises.'

Who can say how, deep downed
they may surface, dancing, when they're most needed
to keep him from drowning.
As they do us now, schooling away.

OGRES AND AUGURS

Now when I really need her the tooth fairy
doesn't come any more to leave a thruppenny joey
or bright tanner under my pillow
augur of a sharp ivory wedge chiselling its way
up from the bone. Instead those childhood ogres
Snaggletooth and Gummy Adams beckon from the shadows.
My sibilants shush like dragged feet through leaf mast
or the tide going out over shingle.
By the time I'm one with Yorick there'll be
hardly a peg for the archaeologists
to hang a date on. My imagination cries 'Pah!'
Yet I've done half as well again as my mother
whose new National Health dentures I gummed
to her forty-year-old jaw with a well-meant
toffee. Yesterday in the news I saw
a mugged man my age dubbed elderly.
But how can that be when I'm reading Goethe
for the first time and this morning, leaving you,
I drove between hills sugared with rime
and hollows brimming with mist white as milk teeth?

TOURIST TALK

Making for the sea the turtle baby
stutters over sandribs barnacle high;
wants to give up; can be deflected
landwards by flotsam of plastic cup
or pebble boulder.
To keep it on course you have to nudge
along, without crushing the soft pouch
of the carapace or the welded toes
tender as frogslegs, that leave
the prints of its progress down
this slipway, ancient before our coming
like bird writing in snow, on the sand behind
the next lather of tide rubs clean
as the live leather coracle floats free.

Making it to the sea
the snagged sled feet unfurl
in a flourish of flippers
slicing away the denser flesh of oceans
joyously buoyant among peers
where we could flounder.
She doesn't look back
driving on out of reach of cavernous cruisers
who would gulp her down.
Given time and luck she'll bring you again
your heart's desire manyfold
when she drags her gravid weight
onto the warm sand to lay down
a new multitude for our nurturing.

NAMING
for Adam Johnson

There's always another Last Romantic.
Playing the tape you gave me now years ago
into this cold grey summer evening of your dying
with Jessye Norman blackly in Strauss
one of life's better ironies
and Mahler's boys jumping out of the bushes
I understand you had to die young
getting better all the time as Keats or even the dear bright faker
Tom Chatterton elegantly slumped
under his garret window, a dangling hand
languid on the floor.

I'm writing in anger of course, at loss, at waste
shedding hard, dry-point tears on this page
for a poet fucked to death, not just
by the moth hands on the heath, magicked
under lamplight and the kissing, keening
canopy of leaves, but by the dogstar
at your birth that spelled a constant seeking
whose end you already half knew could only come
in words spilt on the paper sheets
not the soft touch, hard thrust of brief encounters.

I look up that Stalybridge you had to come from
on the edge of city and moor, a lot like Hampstead.
The hedges are veiled with lace of cow parsley
and deathly May for the marriage of another
virgin Spring you didn't live to see.
No shabby old skin overcoat for you.
There in the bed you were thirteen again
your flesh like a child's pearled and smooth
your face gone back to tender jailbait.

In those last minutes before the cruel
bell rang you in, you honed the art of naming
things and places and taught us with your passion
against the grain, how poetry still matters.